KEEP THEM SAFE

n Educator's Guide to School Safety, Digital Safety, and Personal Safety

To: ________________________________

From: ______________________________

Dr. Raymond Trigg

ISBN: 9798869056948
Trigg, Raymond

Keep Them Safe: An Educator's Guide to School Safety, Digital Safety, and Personal Safety

© Copyright 2023 - All rights reserved.

Cover Design & Layout:

Kantis Simmons, The SIMAKAN Group

"In **Keep Them Safe: An Educator's Guide to School Safety, Digital Safety, and Personal Safety**, Dr. Raymond Trigg, a seasoned retired police officer with a profound dedication to education and self-awareness, offers a comprehensive resource for educators seeking to prioritize personal safety and protect students and young adults in diverse situations.

With a focus on **awareness**, **proactive decision-making**, and **personal responsibility**, this book empowers teenagers with a comprehensive understanding of safety and life skills needed to navigate the complexities of the modern world. It aims to ensure that teens succeed and stay safe in today's dynamic environment. By providing insights into physical well-being, digital savvy, conflict resolution, and personal protection, this guide prepares teenagers to make informed choices and prioritize safety across various aspects of their lives.

This book equips educators, parents, and guardians with the **tools to help students make informed, safe choices**. With insights from responsible online behavior to conflict resolution and personal protection, it aims to shape a generation prioritizing safety in all aspects of life. In today's dynamic environment, safety is a shared responsibility, and this guide encourages collaboration between educators, parents, guardians, and communities to ensure that students thrive while feeling secure.

KEEP THEM SAFE

Introduction:

Welcome to **"Keep Them Safe: An Educator's Guide to School Safety, Digital Safety, and Personal Safety."**

In today's rapidly evolving world, education extends far beyond imparting knowledge; it encompasses the responsibility of safeguarding our students' well-being and empowering them with the skills to navigate various challenges.

This comprehensive guide is divided into three essential sections, each dedicated to a critical aspect of safety:

Part 1 – School Safety

In this section, we explore the vital domain of school safety and emergency preparedness. Educators are not only entrusted with shaping young minds but also with ensuring their physical and emotional security. From understanding potential emergencies to crafting effective emergency response plans, these 26 tips provide educators with the tools to instill confidence and resilience in times of crisis.

Part 2 – Digital Safety

The digital age presents both opportunities and risks for today's youth. As educators, our role extends to cultivating responsible digital citizens who can harness technology's power while maintaining their well-being. Through 25 indispensable tips, we guide educators in teaching digital wisdom, privacy protection, and ethical behavior in the digital space.

Part 3 – Personal Safety

Our duty to students encompasses not only academic growth but also nurturing their personal safety and resilience. This section offers 25 invaluable tips to empower students with comprehensive personal safety skills. From physical well-being to conflict resolution, these insights equip students to confidently navigate the complexities of life.

As you embark on this journey, remember that safety is a collaborative effort involving educators, parents, guardians, and the community. By embracing these principles, we aspire to create a generation that is not only knowledgeable but also prepared, aware, and empowered to face the world with confidence.

Join me in the pursuit of a safer and more secure future for our students – one where knowledge, compassion, and safety intersect to shape a brighter tomorrow.

SCHOOL SAFETY

PART 1

Part 1 – School Safety

In the realm of education, our primary objective is to foster an environment where students can learn, grow, and thrive. However, the landscape of today's world demands more from educators than just imparting knowledge. It calls for a keen sense of responsibility toward the safety and well-being of every student under our care.

As we embark on this section of "Keep Them Safe: An Educator's Guide to School Safety, Digital Safety, and Personal Safety," we delve into a collection of 26 essential tips designed to empower educators in the critical domain of School Safety and emergency preparedness.

From understanding potential emergencies to mastering the intricate threads of an emergency response plan, these tips are meticulously crafted to arm educators with the tools they need to navigate crises with confidence and poise. In a rapidly changing world, educators must possess the skills to instruct and the knowledge to protect.

Our multi-faceted approach encompasses the technical aspects of emergency drills and procedures and the emotional intelligence required to address students' fears and concerns. It's about mastering effective communication, nurturing a survival mindset, and promoting a safe and inclusive learning environment where every student feels secure.

Throughout these pages, you'll encounter strategies that range from practicing emergency drills to fostering open lines of communication with students. We explore the significance of up-to-date first aid and CPR knowledge, the importance of designated rally points, and the power of trusting instincts in the face of uncertainty.

While these tips guide educators, it's essential to remember that school safety is a collaborative effort. Administrators, support staff, parents, and the community at large all play pivotal roles in maintaining a secure educational environment.

As you navigate these 26 tips, envision how each can seamlessly integrate into your educational practices. Consider the broader impact of your actions on students' lives and well-being. By embracing these principles, we strive to create a generation of educators who impart knowledge and embody the values of preparedness, safety, and compassion.

My mission is clear: to empower educators to stand as pillars of strength in times of crisis, champion their students' safety, and foster an environment where learning can thrive in an atmosphere of security and assurance.

Let's embark on this journey of empowerment and enlightenment, equipping ourselves with the wisdom and skills needed to keep our schools safe and our students thriving.

1. Understanding Potential Emergencies: Empowering Teachers for Effective Response and Preparedness

It is of utmost importance for teachers to have a comprehensive understanding of potential school emergencies that could threaten students. By being well-informed, teachers can prioritize student safety, respond swiftly to emergencies, and minimize panic and confusion.

Their knowledge allows for timely and coordinated action, both independently and in collaboration with authorities, ensuring a more effective and efficient response.

Additionally, understanding potential emergencies empowers teachers to take preventive measures, identify areas of vulnerability, and implement appropriate safety protocols. By educating and preparing students, teachers equip them with the necessary skills and knowledge to protect themselves during emergencies.

Furthermore, teachers' awareness of potential risks enables them to provide emotional support, assess and address vulnerabilities, facilitate communication and collaboration among stakeholders, and create a secure learning environment conducive to student well-being.

2. Mastering the Emergency Response Plan: Empowering Teachers for Effective Preparedness and Student Safety

Understanding the school's emergency response plan is crucial for teachers to respond to various situations effectively. This understanding includes knowing evacuation routes, designated safe zones, and procedures for different emergencies. By being familiar with the emergency response plan, teachers can ensure preparedness in the following ways:

Preparedness: Knowing the emergency response plan prepares teachers for potential emergencies. Understanding the procedures and protocols allows them to respond quickly and effectively, minimizing panic and confusion.

Student Safety: Teachers' primary responsibility is their students' safety and well-being. Understanding the emergency response plan enables teachers to make informed decisions during critical situations, ensuring the safety of their students.

Additionally, **Clear Communication** is vital in an emergency. Teachers familiar with the emergency response plan can effectively communicate instructions to students, helping them understand what to do and where to go. This communication helps maintain order and facilitates a coordinated response, ultimately contributing to the overall safety of everyone involved.

3. Navigating Safety: Empowering Teachers through Building Familiarity in Emergencies

Teachers must be familiar with their school building in the event of a school emergency for several reasons. First and foremost, knowing the layout of the building enables teachers to navigate quickly and efficiently, leading students to safety during an evacuation or lockdown. Being familiar with emergency exits, alternative routes, and designated safe areas allows teachers to make informed decisions and take appropriate actions to protect their students.

Additionally, teachers who are knowledgeable about the building can effectively communicate instructions to students during an emergency. Clear communication is vital for maintaining order and ensuring a coordinated response. By understanding the layout and features of the building, teachers can guide students to the nearest exits or safe zones, minimizing panic and confusion.

Furthermore, familiarity with the building enhances teachers' ability to identify potential hazards or safety concerns. They can quickly recognize blocked exits, malfunctioning equipment, or other risks that may threaten student safety. This familiarity allows teachers to take immediate action, report the issues to the appropriate authorities, and implement necessary measures to mitigate risks.

4. Anticipating Emergencies: The Power of "What If" Questions in Teacher Preparedness

When dealing with school emergencies, asking yourself "what if" questions is essential for teachers. This approach serves multiple purposes and offers valuable benefits. Firstly, it promotes preparedness by encouraging teachers to think through different scenarios and potential challenges they may face during an emergency. By asking "what if" questions, teachers can identify potential risks, assess the adequacy of existing emergency plans, and develop contingency strategies to address unexpected situations. This proactive mindset ensures teachers are mentally prepared and equipped to handle various emergencies.

Asking "what if" questions help teachers enhance their decision-making abilities; it prompts them to consider different options and evaluate the potential outcomes of each course of action. Teachers can make informed decisions in high-stress situations by imagining various scenarios and considering the consequences. This critical thinking skill enables them to respond effectively, minimize panic, and prioritize the safety and well-being of their students.

Additionally, asking "what if" questions fosters a culture of continuous improvement and learning. By regularly evaluating and challenging their emergency preparedness plans, teachers can identify areas for improvement and make necessary adjustments.

This self-reflection process allows them to stay updated with best practices, incorporate new knowledge or resources, and ensure that their emergency response strategies align with their school environment's evolving needs and risks.

5. Practicing for Preparedness: Strengthening Teacher Readiness through Mental and Physical Emergency Drills

Mental practice allows teachers to familiarize themselves with emergency procedures, scenarios, and potential challenges. By mentally rehearsing their plans, teachers can visualize and envision themselves successfully responding to emergencies.

This mental preparation helps build confidence, clarity, and decision-making skills, enabling teachers to act quickly and effectively during high-stress incidents. The mental practice also allows teachers to anticipate and mentally prepare for unexpected events, helping them adapt and make informed decisions.

On the other hand, physical practice involves actively implementing and rehearsing emergency plans through drills, simulations, or training exercises. This practical preparation helps teachers translate their mental preparation into tangible actions.

By physically practicing their techniques, teachers can identify any gaps or weaknesses in their emergency procedures, refine their responses, and improve overall readiness. The physical practice also allows for identifying and resolving logistical issues, such as communication breakdowns, evacuation challenges, or equipment malfunctions. Teachers develop muscle memory through repetition and hands-on experience, enabling them to respond quickly and instinctively during emergencies.

Combining mental and physical practice is vital for teachers in school emergencies. It enhances their preparedness, decision-making abilities, and coordination skills. By actively engaging in both forms of training, teachers can better protect and support their students, create a safe learning environment, and ensure a prompt and effective response in times of crisis.

6. Securing Safety: The Importance of Functional Doors and Windows in School Emergency Preparedness

Firstly, functional doors and windows play a critical role in maintaining the security and safety of students and staff during an emergency. In situations such as lockdowns or active shooter incidents, having doors that can be securely locked and windows that can be properly covered can help create a barrier of protection and prevent unauthorized access. Functional doors and windows provide physical security, allow teachers to implement necessary safety protocols, and for law enforcement to respond.

Secondly, properly functioning doors and windows enable efficient evacuation procedures during emergencies such as fires or natural disasters. In these situations, quick and orderly evacuation is crucial, and any malfunctioning doors or windows can hinder the evacuation process and put lives at risk.

Teachers must ensure that doors can be easily opened and windows can be safely used as exit points if required. Regular maintenance and inspections of doors and windows help identify any issues and allow for prompt repairs or replacements.

7. A Survival Mindset: Empowering Teachers in School Emergency Response

Developing a survival mindset is important for teachers when dealing with school emergencies as it enables them to respond effectively, prioritize safety, and maintain composure. This mindset promotes preparedness by encouraging teachers to anticipate emergencies and be mentally and physically ready to respond. It involves being aware of the specific risks and hazards that can occur in a school setting and taking proactive steps to mitigate those risks. By fostering preparedness, teachers can stay calm, make quick decisions, and take appropriate actions during high-stress situations.

A survival mindset also empowers teachers to act swiftly and decisively in crises. They can effectively assess the situation, evaluate available resources, and implement emergency protocols. This quick and effective response helps minimize panic, confusion, and potential harm.

Additionally, teachers with a survival mindset demonstrate adaptability and problem-solving skills. They can think critically, make necessary adjustments, and find creative solutions to manage unforeseen challenges during an emergency. By cultivating resilience and fostering a supportive environment, teachers can prioritize student safety, provide clear instructions, and instill a sense of calm among their students.

This mindset equips teachers with the mental, emotional, and practical tools to navigate school emergencies, ensuring their students' well-being and the school community's overall security.

8. Empowering Safety: The Role of Proactive Reporting in Maintaining a Secure School Environment

Proactively reporting potential safety threats or suspicious behavior within the school premises is crucial for teachers during emergencies. Promptly reporting such concerns enables swift intervention and preventive measures, allowing for assessing the situation and necessary actions to mitigate risks.

By informing the appropriate authorities immediately, teachers play a vital role in preventing accidents or emergencies from occurring or escalating, thus maintaining a secure learning environment and safeguarding the well-being of students and staff.

This proactive approach contributes to early detection and prevention by leveraging teachers' close interactions with students, as they are well-positioned to identify unusual behavior or signs of potential threats. By promptly reporting suspicious activity, teachers provide valuable information to the authorities, facilitating prompt evaluation and appropriate responses. This early detection enables the identification of potential risks and the implementation of proactive measures to ensure the safety of everyone within the school community.

Furthermore, proactive reporting of safety threats and suspicious behavior sets a positive example for students and fosters a culture of accountability and vigilance. It encourages students to be vigilant, responsible, and actively involved in maintaining a secure environment. When teachers actively report incidents, they demonstrate their commitment to student safety and contribute to the overall well-being of the school community.

This collective effort ensures that the school community remains proactive, prepared, and resilient in potential emergencies. By taking action and reporting concerns, teachers fulfill their role in maintaining safety and inspire students to be proactive and engaged participants in their security.

9. Promoting Safety Through Open Communication: Empowering Students to Report and Prevent Emergencies

Open school communication is crucial for creating a safe and supportive environment, particularly when dealing with safety threats and suspicious activities. By fostering an environment where students feel comfortable expressing concerns or sharing information, teachers can establish trust and open dialogue, which is essential for the early detection and prevention of potential emergencies.

When students feel safe and supported, they are more likely to report any potential threats or suspicious activities they observe or hear about, providing valuable information to teachers. This safety and support enable students to take appropriate actions to address the concerns and ensure the safety of the school community.

Encouraging open communication also empowers students to become active participants in their safety. By teaching them about the importance of reporting and providing them with the necessary channels to do so, teachers empower students to take responsibility for their well-being and that of their peers. This proactive approach helps create a sense of shared responsibility and encourages students to look out for one another. Furthermore, fostering open communication helps to break down barriers and dispel misconceptions.

By addressing concerns and encouraging dialogue, teachers can debunk rumors or address unfounded fears that may circulate among students. This method helps maintain a calm and secure learning environment, promotes accurate information sharing, and prevents unnecessary panic.

10. Promoting a Safe and Inclusive Learning Environment: Monitoring Student Behavior and Addressing Bullying and Harassment

Monitoring student behavior and addressing bullying or harassment is important for teachers regarding school safety for students. By actively observing and intervening in such situations, teachers promote a safe and inclusive learning environment where students feel valued, respected, and protected. It conveys that bullying and harassment are unacceptable and will not be tolerated, creating a supportive school climate.

Addressing bullying and harassment is essential to prevent the negative consequences that can arise from these behaviors. By intervening early, teachers can mitigate the emotional, psychological, and academic impacts on targeted students, ensuring they have equal opportunities to thrive academically and socially.

Additionally, prompt action helps prevent these incidents from escalating into larger safety issues within the school. By addressing and resolving bullying and harassment, teachers contribute to a safe and harmonious environment, reducing the likelihood of more severe disruptions or incidents.

In summary, monitoring student behavior and promptly addressing bullying or harassment is vital for teachers in ensuring school safety for students. By creating a safe and inclusive learning environment, protecting students from harm, and preventing negative consequences, teachers play a crucial role in promoting student well-being and preventing the escalation of safety issues within the school.

11. Maintaining Vital Connections: Staying Updated on Students' Emergency Contacts and Medical Conditions

Having accurate and current emergency contact information allows teachers to contact parents or guardians in an emergency quickly. By promptly notifying parents about the situation, teachers can collaborate to take appropriate actions and provide the necessary support. This open line of communication ensures that parents are involved and informed during critical situations, contributing to the overall safety and security of the students.

Additionally, awareness of students' medical conditions or allergies empowers teachers to provide appropriate care and take preventive measures. This information allows teachers to implement necessary precautions, be aware of prescribed medication, or seek immediate medical assistance when required. This proactive approach enables teachers to respond promptly in case of a medical emergency, ensuring the well-being and health of the students in their care.

By staying updated on students' emergency contact information and relevant medical conditions or allergies, teachers demonstrate their commitment to student safety. It facilitates effective communication, enables timely response, and promotes a secure learning environment where students can thrive. Ultimately, being well-informed allows teachers to prioritize the individual needs of their students and create a supportive educational setting.

12. Readiness in Times of Crisis: Maintaining Essential Emergency Supplies in the Classroom

A well-equipped first aid kit enables teachers to promptly address injuries and provide immediate care until professional help arrives. It allows for quick response and potentially reduces the severity of injuries, promoting faster recovery.

Water and non-perishable snacks are essential supplies during a school emergency. They help address basic needs and provide sustenance when food and water access is limited or restricted. These readily available supplies allow teachers to keep students hydrated, nourished, and comfortable during stressful times. By ensuring access to these essential items, teachers can prioritize the well-being of their students and provide necessary support in challenging situations.

In essence, keeping essential emergency supplies readily available, such as a first aid kit, water, and non-perishable snacks, is crucial for teachers during a school emergency. These supplies enable teachers to respond effectively to injuries and address basic needs. By being well-prepared, teachers can prioritize student safety, well-being, and comfort, contributing to a secure and supportive environment during times of crisis.

13. Understanding the Heroes: Teaching Students about the Role of Emergency Personnel

Firstly, educating students about the role of emergency personnel helps them understand the importance of these professionals in maintaining safety and providing assistance during emergencies. It helps students develop respect and appreciation for emergency personnel's work in protecting and helping the community. Learning about their roles and responsibilities, students better understand how emergency responders contribute to their well-being.

Secondly, teaching students how to interact with emergency personnel during an emergency prepares them to respond appropriately and cooperatively in high-stress situations. Students learn to communicate effectively with emergency personnel, providing them with the necessary information and following their instructions. This knowledge can help students remain calm and cooperative, allowing emergency responders to carry out their duties more efficiently and effectively.

Additionally, educating students about emergency personnel instills a sense of trust and confidence in these professionals. By understanding the roles and responsibilities of firefighters, police officers, and paramedics, students are more likely to feel safe and secure during emergencies. They know that trained professionals are available to help and protect them, which can reduce fear and anxiety in such situations.

14. Emphasizing the importance of listening and following directions from

teachers, administrators, or emergency personnel during drills and real emergencies is crucial for several reasons.

Following directions is essential for maintaining order, ensuring everyone's safety, and facilitating an organized response during drills and emergencies. When students listen to and follow the instructions given by teachers, administrators, or emergency personnel, it helps create a structured environment where necessary actions can be taken promptly and efficiently. This cooperative behavior allows emergency responders to carry out their duties effectively and minimizes confusion or panic among students.

Emphasizing the importance of listening and following directions promotes a culture of preparedness and safety awareness among students. By stressing the significance of these actions, teachers instill a sense of responsibility and accountability in students. They understand that following directions is for their well-being and the well-being of their peers and the entire school community. This mindset encourages students to take drills and real emergencies seriously and actively participate in safety protocols. In summary, emphasizing the importance of listening and following directions from teachers, administrators, or emergency personnel during drills and real emergencies is essential.

15. Maintaining Life-Saving Skills: The Significance of Current First Aid, CPR, and AED Knowledge

Emergencies can occur at any time and place, including within the school environment. By regularly refreshing their knowledge and skills in first aid, CPR, and AED procedures, teachers can be prepared to provide immediate assistance when needed. Prompt and effective action can significantly affect the outcome in critical situations such as cardiac arrest or severe injuries. Having up-to-date knowledge allows teachers to respond confidently and potentially save lives.

Staying current with first aid, CPR, and AED procedures demonstrates a commitment to the safety and well-being of students. It shows that teachers take their responsibilities seriously and are dedicated to being capable first responders in emergencies. This commitment inspires confidence among students, parents, and the school community, knowing that there are trained individuals who can provide immediate assistance if an emergency occurs.

Regularly reviewing and updating knowledge in these areas enables teachers to adapt to any advancements or protocol changes. Best practices in emergency response continually evolve, and teachers must stay informed of new techniques or guidelines. Teachers can ensure they employ the most effective and evidence-based approaches when providing immediate emergency assistance by staying up-to-date.

16. Promoting Focus and Safety: Ensuring Compliance with Electronic Device Policies during School Emergencies

Teachers must understand and enforce the school's electronic device usage policies during emergencies. They maintain a calm and controlled environment, free from panic and misinformation. Teachers ensure accurate information is communicated through official channels, minimizing confusion and fear. Enforcing guidelines also prevents distractions that divert students' attention from important instructions and safety protocols. It allows students to remain focused and responsive and prioritize their safety during critical situations.

Consistent enforcement of policies on personal electronic devices promotes a sense of order, discipline, and respect for rules within the school community. It establishes clear expectations for behavior during emergencies and emphasizes responsible and respectful use of technology. By adhering to these guidelines, teachers contribute to a safer and more organized environment where everyone understands their role in maintaining the overall safety and well-being of the school community. Ultimately, understanding and enforcing these policies help create a climate conducive to effective emergency response, accurate information dissemination, and responsible use of technology.

17. Equipping Students with Life-Saving Skills: Teaching Emergency Response Procedures for Evacuation, Lockdown, and Shelter-in-Place

Teaching students specific emergency response procedures and conducting regular drills are vital for their safety and preparedness. By familiarizing students with evacuation routes, lockdown protocols, and shelter-in-place instructions, teachers empower them to respond effectively during crises. Regular drills provide practical experience, reinforcing students' understanding and enabling them to act quickly and confidently in high-stress situations.

These drills help students practice the necessary actions and identify areas for improvement in emergency procedures. Teachers can observe students' behavior, address misconceptions, and refine the response strategies accordingly. Additionally, the drills promote teamwork and collective responsibility among students, fostering a culture of preparedness and unity.

In summary, teaching emergency response procedures and conducting regular drills enhance students' safety and preparedness. By equipping them with knowledge, providing practical experience, and promoting teamwork, teachers ensure that students can respond effectively during emergencies, contributing to a safer learning environment.

18. Preparing Students for Emergency Situations: Recognizing and Responding to School Alarms and Instructions

Teachers have to ensure the safety and well-being of students; it is important to teach them how to recognize and respond to different instructions, emergency signals, or alarms used within the school environment. By equipping students with the knowledge and skills to accurately interpret and act upon these signals, they can play an active role in their safety and contribute to a secure school community.

Teaching students to recognize and understand different instructions and signals prepares them to communicate effectively during emergencies. Whether it's a fire alarm or a lockdown alert, students familiar with the meaning and appropriate responses to these signals can assist in maintaining a calm and organized atmosphere. By providing students with the necessary knowledge, teachers empower them to respond promptly and follow safety protocols, ultimately enhancing communication and minimizing confusion during critical situations.

19. Addressing Misconceptions and Alleviating Fears: Providing Accurate Information on Emergencies while Dispelling Rumors and Myths for Students

Addressing any misconceptions or fears that students may have about emergencies is an important responsibility for teachers. Teachers can promote a sense of calm, understanding, and preparedness among students by providing accurate information and dispelling rumors or myths.

Misconceptions and fears can lead to unnecessary panic or inappropriate responses during emergencies. By addressing these concerns, teachers can help students develop a realistic understanding of emergencies and the appropriate actions. This knowledge reduces anxiety and empowers students to respond effectively, ensuring their safety and the safety of others.

Moreover, providing accurate information helps prevent the spreading of rumors or misinformation. During emergencies, inaccurate information can create unnecessary chaos and confusion, hindering response efforts. By dispelling rumors and providing accurate information, teachers can maintain order and ensure students have reliable information to guide their actions.

By addressing misconceptions and fears, teachers foster an atmosphere of trust and confidence among students. This proactive approach ensures that students' concerns are acknowledged and provides them with reliable and accurate information from their teachers. Consequently, students feel reassured, knowing they can rely on their teachers for guidance and support. This sense of security cultivates a calm and focused response during emergencies, empowering students to navigate such circumstances with composure and resilience.

In summary, addressing misconceptions and fears about emergencies is crucial for teachers. Teachers can reduce anxiety, promote effective responses, and maintain order during critical situations by providing accurate information and dispelling rumors. This proactive approach helps students develop a realistic understanding of emergencies and empowers them to take appropriate actions to ensure their safety.

20. Navigating Emotions in Emergencies: Supporting Students' Emotional Well-being during Drills and Crisis Situations

During drills and actual emergencies, students may experience a range of emotional reactions, including fear, anxiety, confusion, and stress. Teachers need to understand and address these potential emotional responses while emphasizing the importance of staying calm and reassuring each other.

Students may feel fearful or anxious during drills and emergencies due to the unfamiliarity of the situation and the perceived threat to their safety. They may also experience confusion and stress as they navigate the protocols and procedures being followed. Teachers must create a supportive and reassuring environment during these times.

Staying calm and composed is essential for teachers as it sets a positive example for students. When students see their teacher remaining calm and collected, it helps to alleviate their fears and anxieties. Teachers can provide clear instructions, use reassuring words, and demonstrate confidence in following emergency protocols. This calm helps to instill a sense of safety and security in students.

Additionally, staying calm and reassuring each other helps students make better decisions and follow emergency procedures effectively. When emotions are heightened, it is easy for students to become overwhelmed or act impulsively. Teachers can help students think more clearly and respond rationally by maintaining a calm environment.

21.Nurturing Preparedness through Ongoing Emergency Procedure Discussions and Clarifications

Regularly discussing and reviewing emergency procedures and expectations with students is crucial in keeping them safe during emergencies. By providing opportunities for students to ask questions and seek clarification, teachers ensure that students clearly understand what to do in different emergencies.

When students are familiar with emergency procedures, they are better prepared to respond appropriately during an actual emergency. Regular discussions and reviews help reinforce important information, such as evacuation routes, lockdown protocols, or shelter-in-place instructions. This familiarity enables students to act quickly and confidently, reducing the risk of confusion or panic.

Allowing students to ask questions and seek clarification helps address any uncertainties or misconceptions they may have. Students may have specific concerns or scenarios they want to understand better, and providing a safe space for them to ask questions promotes a sense of trust and open communication. By addressing these questions, teachers can ensure that students have accurate information and a clear understanding of what is expected of them during emergencies.

Moreover, regular discussions and reviews of emergency procedures create a culture of preparedness and vigilance among students. It reinforces the importance of taking emergencies seriously and encourages a proactive mindset. Students become more aware of their surroundings, potential hazards, and the necessary steps to ensure their safety.

Teachers empower students with knowledge, clarity, and confidence by regularly discussing and reviewing emergency procedures. This proactive approach enhances student safety by ensuring they are well-informed, prepared, and equipped to respond effectively during emergencies.

22.Mastering Communication Tools for Effective Emergency Response and Collaboration

During emergencies or critical situations, clear and timely communication is crucial. Teachers must be familiar with the available communication tools and understand how to utilize them effectively. This familiarity includes knowing how to operate the public address system to broadcast important announcements or instructions to students and staff. It also involves proficiently using classroom phones, mobile phones, or communication apps to relay information or seek emergency assistance when needed.

Having a firm command of these communication tools allows teachers to swiftly and effectively share vital information with students, staff, and other pertinent stakeholders during emergencies. This capability ensures that critical instructions, updates, or guidance reach everyone promptly, fostering a coordinated response and bolstering overall safety measures.

In addition, being well-versed in these communication tools enables teachers to establish and maintain vital connections within the school district. They can seamlessly communicate effectively with colleagues, administrators, and support staff, fostering the exchange of relevant information and collaborative efforts during emergency response. This proactive approach promotes a unified and coordinated approach to handling emergencies, amplifying the effectiveness of the response. This knowledge empowers teachers to communicate efficiently during emergencies, promptly ensuring crucial information reaches all stakeholders. By effectively leveraging these tools, teachers contribute to cultivating a safer and more interconnected school environment.

23. The Importance of Location Awareness for Teachers

Knowing the exact location and room number of the room they are assigned to and any alternate or temporary locations is crucial for teachers during a school emergency for effective communication and swift response.

If teachers are not in their main room, such as during a class change or an off-site activity, knowing the exact location and room number allows them to inform emergency responders or school administrators quickly. This information helps direct the appropriate assistance to the specific area of concern, minimizing response time and ensuring a more targeted and efficient approach.

Furthermore, knowing the room number enables teachers to communicate their location to other staff members or colleagues. Clear and accurate communication is vital for coordinating actions, sharing information, and receiving instructions during an emergency. Teachers can help facilitate effective communication by providing the room number and ensuring that the right support and resources are promptly directed to their location.

24. The Importance of Designated Rally Points: Ensuring Accountability, Safety, and Effective Communication in School Emergencies

Knowing the designated rally point or meet-up spot in an evacuation is important for teachers as it facilitates accountability, safety, and effective communication during a school emergency.

Designating a pre-determined rally point is vital in emergency evacuations as it provides teachers and students with a centralized location to gather and regroup. This strategic measure serves the crucial purpose of accounting for everyone, guaranteeing that no individual is left behind or unaccounted for amidst the chaos of an evacuation. By clearly understanding the rally point, teachers can swiftly guide their students to the designated area, minimizing confusion and instilling a systematic approach to account for the entire class or group. This organized response not only ensures the safety of all individuals but also brings a sense of order and efficiency to the evacuation process.

Moreover, the rally point is a central communication hub during an emergency. Teachers can relay important information, updates, or instructions to their students and fellow staff members at the rally point. It provides a focal point for communication with emergency personnel, administrators, or other response teams, facilitating coordination and disseminating crucial information. By gathering at the designated rally point, teachers can help ensure everyone receives necessary instructions and updates, enhancing safety and situational awareness.

25. The Significance of Students Knowing the Designated Rally Point: Enhancing Security, Accountability, and Communication in Emergencies

For several reasons, students need to know the designated rally point or meet-up spot in the event of an evacuation or emergency. First and foremost, knowing the rally point provides students with a sense of security and direction during a potentially chaotic situation. Knowing the rally point allows students to go to the designated location independently if disconnected from their class or teacher. This information reduces panic, uncertainty, and the risk of wandering off or becoming disoriented.

The rally point serves as a central gathering point for accountability and communication. If a student becomes disconnected from their class, teachers can effortlessly confirm their presence upon their arrival at the rally point. This proactive measure guarantees that no student is inadvertently left behind or placed in an unsafe location, prioritizing their well-being and safety. Additionally, at the rally point, students can receive further instructions, updates, or assistance from their teachers, administrators, or emergency personnel. It serves as a hub for communication, ensuring that disconnected students are informed and included in the overall response and safety measures.

26. Empowering Teachers: The Importance of Trusting Instincts for Student Safety and Well-being

Trust your instincts and intuition regarding personal safety. If something feels unsafe, taking it seriously and seeking assistance is important.

Trusting instincts are crucial for teachers in keeping students safe in schools. It allows them to detect potential risks, respond promptly to emergencies, enhance situational awareness, build personal connections with students, and take a proactive approach to safety. By relying on their instincts; teachers can quickly recognize and address safety concerns, make informed decisions during emergencies, and maintain a secure learning environment for their students.

Trusting instincts also enables teachers to establish stronger connections with students, being attentive to their individual needs and well-being. It helps teachers anticipate and address potential risks, fostering a proactive approach to student safety. By trusting their instincts, teachers become active participants in maintaining a safe school environment, protecting students from harm, and ensuring a conducive learning environment for their overall well-being.

DIGITAL SAFETY

PART 2

Part 2 – Digital Safety

Keep Them Safe: An Educators Guide to Digital Safety: Cultivating Digital Wisdom in a Hyperconnected World

In an age of connectivity and instant access to information, the digital landscape presents opportunities and challenges for today's youth. As educators, we must guide them in harnessing the power of technology while fostering a strong sense of responsibility and digital citizenship. In this section of "Keep Them Safe: An Educator's Guide to School Safety, Digital Safety, and Personal Safety," we delve into a collection of 25 indispensable tips that address the dynamic realm of Digital Safety and digital citizenship.

Digital wisdom is not merely about mastering technology; it's about nurturing a holistic understanding of how our actions in the digital space can impact our lives and the lives of others. From responsible online behavior to protecting personal information, from guarding against cyberbullying to cultivating a healthy relationship with technology, these tips offer a comprehensive toolkit for educators to impart essential lessons to their students.

As we embark on this journey, we will navigate various concepts intricately connected to the dynamic modern digital landscape. Our exploration will delve into the nuances of privacy settings and the significance of crafting strong passwords, both pivotal in safeguarding personal information. We will dive into the realm of online content creation, examining its creative potential while emphasizing the responsibility of being a digital citizen. Moreover, we will address the profound impact of social media on mental health and well-being, highlighting the importance of striking a balance in this technology-driven era.

While these tips are designed to guide students, they also underscore educators' critical role in setting an example. A teacher who practices responsible cell phone use and digital etiquette is a role model for students, highlighting the intersection of technology and ethical behavior.

In today's interconnected world, the digital realm knows no boundaries. It's not confined to classrooms or school hours; it's a part of our students' lives around the clock. Thus, the responsibility of fostering digital wisdom transcends traditional educational settings. It calls for collaboration with parents, guardians, and the community.

Through this journey, consider how each Tip can be woven into the fabric of your educational approach. Reflect on the profound influence educators have in shaping the digital mindset of students. By embracing these principles, we aim to cultivate a generation of digital citizens who engage thoughtfully, contribute positively, and navigate the online world with wisdom and discernment.

My mission is clear: to empower students to become responsible stewards of the digital realm, to equip them with the tools to protect their well-being and privacy, and to foster an online environment that mirrors the values of respect, empathy, and collaboration. Let's embark on this expedition of digital exploration and empowerment, ushering in a future where technology is a force for good, and our students are its torchbearers.

1. Digital Citizenship: Nurturing Responsible Online Behavior and Empowering Digital Citizens.

Teach students about digital citizenship rights and responsibilities, including online safety and ethical behavior.

Digital citizenship refers to the responsible, ethical, and safe use of technology and digital platforms. It encompasses a set of skills and behaviors that individuals need to navigate the digital world effectively. As a teacher, starting with digital citizenship sets the foundation for teaching students about online safety and responsible cell phone and social media use.

By starting with digital citizenship, teachers can provide a comprehensive framework for teaching students about online safety, responsible cell phone and social media use, and ethical behavior in the digital world. It empowers students to become accountable and mindful digital citizens who confidently make informed choices and navigate the digital landscape.

2. Setting the Stage for Digital Responsibility: Establishing Guidelines for Safe and Ethical Cell Phone and Social Media Use

In today's digital age, it is essential to establish clear guidelines for safe and responsible cell phone and social media use. By setting these rules and expectations in the classroom, educators create a secure and controlled environment for students to engage with technology. These guidelines help students understand the boundaries and responsibilities that come with online behavior, promoting digital literacy and responsible digital citizenship. By teaching students, the importance of digital ethics and safety, educators equip them with the necessary skills to navigate the digital world with integrity and protect themselves from potential online risks.

Furthermore, fostering a supportive classroom environment is paramount in cultivating healthy digital habits. Creating a safe space where students can openly discuss online challenges, seek guidance, and support one another is crucial. By encouraging open dialogue, educators empower students to share their concerns and seek assistance when navigating digital spaces. This supportive atmosphere promotes collaboration and empathy, allowing students to learn from each other's experiences and develop critical thinking skills. By addressing digital challenges collectively, students gain resilience and are better equipped to make responsible decisions online, contributing to a positive and inclusive digital community.

3. Guarding Your Device: Teaching Students to Protect Against Physical Theft and Safeguard Personal Information

Teach students to be mindful of their surroundings and to keep their cell phones secure to prevent physical theft. Advise them to avoid leaving their devices unattended in public places and to store them securely when not in use. Teach students the basics of keeping their devices secure, such as installing updates and enabling device lock features like passcodes or biometric authentication. It's also crucial to activate device tracking features such as 'Find My Phone' and remotely wipe or lock their devices if lost or stolen. It is also important to be vigilant in public spaces and keep the phone secure and out of sight when not in use.

Physical theft of cell phones can have severe consequences, including financial fraud, where thieves exploit sensitive information stored on the device to gain unauthorized access to bank accounts, credit cards, or online payment platforms. Moreover, stolen cell phones can provide access to personal data, such as emails, social media accounts, and private messages, leading to privacy breaches and potential identity theft.

Unauthorized access to social media accounts can further exacerbate the situation, as it creates opportunities for cyberbullying. By gaining access to personal profiles, bullies can manipulate and misuse private information, leading to online harassment and emotional distress. By instilling the habit of mindful cell phone security, teachers can help students proactively protect themselves against the serious consequences that may arise from physical theft.

4. Secure Your Screen: Empowering Students with Screen Lock for Enhanced Mobile Device Security

Encourage students to enable the screen lock feature on their cell phones, such as PIN, pattern, or biometric authentication (e.g., fingerprint or face recognition). Emphasize the importance of locking their devices whenever they are not in use.

Enabling a screen lock on smartphones is crucial as it provides a layer of security, privacy protection, and data security. By setting up a screen lock, individuals prevent unauthorized access to personal information, sensitive data, and potentially malicious activities in case of phone loss or theft. Additionally, a locked device ensures the privacy of personal conversations, social media accounts, emails, photos, and other private content, safeguarding them from being accessed by unauthorized individuals. In the unfortunate event of a security breach or device theft, a screen lock is a barrier against unauthorized data access, minimizing the risk of identity theft, financial fraud, or misuse of personal information.

5. Guarding Your Digital Footprint: Empowering Students through Privacy Settings and Strong Passwords

Promoting privacy and responsible use of social media involves educating students on privacy settings and keeping personal information private. By teaching students how to navigate and adjust privacy settings on social media platforms, they can control who can see their posts and access their personal information. Understanding the available privacy settings empowers students to make informed decisions about their online presence. It is crucial to emphasize the importance of keeping personal information confidential, such as avoiding sharing full names, addresses, phone numbers, or other sensitive details online.

By combining these efforts, students can develop a strong awareness of privacy and actively protect their personal information while engaging in online platforms.

6. Fortifying Your Digital Fortress: Empowering Students through Strong and Unique Passwords

Teach students the importance of creating strong passwords for their accounts and using different passwords for each platform. Strong and unique passwords are crucial for maintaining online security and protecting personal information. Strong passwords are a barrier against unauthorized access, making it more difficult for hackers to guess or crack passwords. They safeguard personal information, reducing the risk of identity theft, fraud, or data misuse.

Additionally, using different passwords for each account mitigates the impact of data breaches, as compromised login credentials on one platform won't compromise other accounts. Strong passwords also protect against brute-force attacks, where attackers systematically try different password combinations. Using strong passwords with a combination of uppercase and lowercase letters, numbers, and symbols makes it significantly more challenging for attackers to guess the password through these methods. Combining strong passwords with additional security measures like two-factor authentication enhances account security. By encouraging students to use strong and unique passwords, we instill good security practices and emphasize the importance of protecting their online presence and personal information.

7. Guarding Your Digital Footprint: Navigating Location Sharing for Personal Safety and Privacy

Being cautious with location sharing is crucial for maintaining personal safety and privacy. Sharing location information through apps or social media platforms can have various implications, such as exposing one's whereabouts and daily routines to a wide audience, including strangers. This information can be exploited to track individuals, monitor their movements, or facilitate stalking and harassment.

It's important to discuss the potential risks of sharing real-time location data with strangers and encourage students to be cautious when enabling location services. Constantly sharing location information increases the likelihood of unwanted contact, invasion of privacy, and compromises personal safety. Students should review privacy settings, adjust permissions, and limit location data sharing with trusted individuals to minimize these risks.

Additionally, pictures can inadvertently reveal location details. Geotagging, a feature available on many smartphones and cameras, embeds location data into the photo's metadata. When sharing images online, others can access this metadata, disclosing the exact location where the photo was taken. Educating students about the risks associated with sharing pictures is crucial, encouraging them to turn off geotagging or carefully consider what information they're unintentionally sharing.

By raising awareness about these risks, students can better understand their online privacy and the potential consequences of sharing location-related information. Empowering students to make informed decisions about their location-sharing practices helps protect their personal safety and privacy in the digital world.

8. Picturing Privacy: Nurturing Responsible Visual Sharing for Personal Safety and Digital Ethics

Being mindful of photos and videos is essential in maintaining personal privacy and preventing the unauthorized sharing of visual content. Students should understand the importance of obtaining consent before sharing photos or videos of themselves or others, respecting personal boundaries, and ensuring everyone involved is comfortable sharing their images.

Emphasize the potential long-term consequences of sharing compromising or inappropriate visuals, as they can impact future opportunities and relationships. Help students recognize that anything shared online can have a lasting digital footprint, and it can be challenging to remove content once it's posted completely. Encourage them to review and adjust their privacy settings on social media platforms to control who can see their posts and restrict the visibility of their photos and videos.

Teaching students about public versus private sharing will teach them to be cautious about sharing personal visuals in public online spaces where they may not have control over who views or shares their content. Encourage them to consider private sharing options with trusted friends or family members. Additionally, stress the importance of respecting the intellectual property and privacy of others by not sharing or reposting someone else's content without permission, and teach them to give credit and obtain consent when sharing content created by others.

9. Empowering Digital Guardians: Reporting Inappropriate Content for a Safer Online Community

Teachers must instruct students to report any inappropriate or harmful content they may encounter on social media platforms. Reporting inappropriate or harmful content is crucial for maintaining a safe and positive online environment. Students need to understand what constitutes such content, including cyberbullying, hate speech, and explicit or violent imagery. By reporting this content, they help protect themselves and others from potential harm, prevent the perpetuation of negativity, and contribute to a healthier online culture.

Students should be encouraged to contact trusted adults such as parents, teachers, or school counselors when they encounter inappropriate content. These individuals are there to provide guidance and support in navigating online challenges. Students should also be aware of the reporting mechanisms available on social media platforms and understand how to utilize these tools effectively. It's important to stress the confidentiality and anonymity of reporting, assuring students that their identities will be protected. Taking screenshots or collecting evidence of inappropriate content can be helpful in investigations or disciplinary actions. By reporting incidents, students become responsible digital citizens and actively contribute to creating a positive and safe online environment for everyone.

Reporting inappropriate or harmful content is crucial in fostering a positive online environment. Students should understand the importance of reporting, know who they can turn to for support, be familiar with reporting mechanisms on social media platforms, and practice responsible digital citizenship. By taking these steps, students can help shape a safer and more inclusive online community, which ultimately benefits their well-being and the well-being of others.

10. Standing Up to Cyberbullying: Empowering Students to Recognize and Report Online Harassment

Teach students how to identify cyberbullying and encourage them to report such incidents to a trusted adult. Cyberbullying refers to using digital platforms to harass, intimidate, or target someone repeatedly. It can manifest through hurtful messages, rumors, embarrassing media sharing, or fake profiles. Students should be aware of signs such as behavior changes, social withdrawal, or declining academic performance.

Encourage them to report cyberbullying incidents to trusted adults, assuring them that action will be taken. Statistics show that around 37% of young people in the United States have experienced cyberbullying.[1] Cyberbullying can have severe consequences, including emotional distress, anxiety, depression, and self-harm. Recognizing cyberbullying, teaching reporting mechanisms, and fostering empathy and digital responsibility can create a safer and more inclusive online environment for everyone.

1. Patchin, Ph.D., Justin. "2019 Cyberbullying Data." Accessed August 15, 2023, https://cyberbullying.org/2019-cyberbullying-data

11. Promoting Responsible Downloading: Safeguarding Device Security and Personal Information

Encouraging responsible downloading is crucial to maintaining device security and protecting personal information. Students should understand the significance of obtaining apps and files exclusively from reputable sources like the Apple App Store or Google Play Store. Emphasize the risks of downloading pirated or unofficial apps, as they may contain malware or compromise device security.

Students can safeguard their devices and personal information by teaching safe downloading practices, such as avoiding potentially harmful or malicious downloads, ensuring a safer and more secure digital experience. Use discretion when accepting app permissions: Instruct students to carefully review app permissions before granting access to personal information or device features.

12. Stay Secure: The Importance of Keeping Devices and Software Updated

Instruct students to regularly update their devices and apps to ensure they have the latest security patches and bug fixes.

Updating devices and software is crucial for maintaining a secure and reliable digital experience. Regular updates provide important security patches, bug fixes, and performance improvements that help protect against cyber threats and vulnerabilities. By instructing students to stay on top of updates, you empower them to safeguard their devices and data proactively. Emphasize the importance of enabling automatic updates or regularly checking for updates manually. This step ensures that students have the latest features, enhancements, and security measures installed on their devices, reducing the risk of exploitation by malicious actors. Students can enhance their digital security, optimize device performance, and ensure a safer and more enjoyable technology experience by cultivating a habit of device and software updates.

13. Stay Skeptical: Navigating Online Offers and Giveaways Safely

Being skeptical of online offers or giveaways is crucial for online safety. Students should exercise caution when encountering offers that seem too good to be true, as they may be potential scams. Online scammers often use attractive offers or giveaways to trick individuals into revealing personal information or downloading malicious software.

Teach students to critically evaluate offers, assess their realism, and research their legitimacy before participating. They should be wary of unrealistic claims and verify the credibility of the company or organization offering the promotion.

Emphasize the importance of protecting personal information and only relying on trusted sources when participating in online offers or giveaways.

By fostering skepticism, students can protect themselves from scams, safeguard their personal information, and make informed decisions online.

14. Finding Balance: Taking Breaks from Technology for Well-being

Encourage students to have regular breaks from their phones and social media to maintain a healthy balance and protect their well-being.

Promoting a healthy balance between technology and real-life experiences is essential for students' well-being. Encouraging regular breaks from phones and social media helps students maintain a healthy relationship with technology and protect their overall well-being. Additionally, it is important to raise awareness about the distractions posed by digital devices and emphasize the importance of managing screen time to stay focused on studies and meaningful face-to-face interactions.

Digital addiction is a growing concern with potentially serious consequences for mental health. Research has shown that a significant percentage of adolescents experience smartphone addiction, and many teenagers feel addicted to their mobile devices. Excessive internet use has been linked to symptoms of depression and anxiety among young people. Moreover, heavy social media use can disrupt sleep patterns and lead to fatigue, while the mere presence of smartphones can negatively impact academic performance. It is crucial to educate students about the signs of digital addiction and provide strategies for maintaining a healthy balance between online and offline activities.

15. Mindful Online Presence: Understanding the Impact of Your Digital Footprint

Teach students about the permanence of their online activities and how their digital footprint can affect their future opportunities.

Educating students about their digital footprint and the long-term implications of their online activities is essential. By being mindful of what they post and share, students can understand how their digital presence can impact future opportunities, such as college admissions or job applications. Additionally, teaching students about safe online communication is crucial for fostering positive and respectful interactions. Emphasizing the importance of appropriate language and tone and avoiding misunderstandings helps students navigate online spaces responsibly and promotes healthy digital citizenship. By combining these lessons, we empower students to make informed decisions about their online presence and equip them with the skills to communicate effectively and respectfully in the digital world.

16.Speak Up, Stay Safe: The Importance of Seeking Help from Trusted Adults Online

Remind students to seek help from a trusted adult if they feel uncomfortable, threatened, or encounter any concerning situations online.

Encouraging students to contact a trusted adult is vital to their online safety. Remind them that if they ever feel uncomfortable, threatened, or encounter any concerning situations online, they should not hesitate to seek help. Trusted adults, such as parents, teachers, or school counselors, can provide guidance, support, and assistance in navigating challenging online experiences. By fostering an open line of communication and emphasizing the importance of seeking help, we empower students to protect themselves and address any issues they may encounter online.

Together, we can create a safe and supportive environment where students feel confident contacting trusted adults for assistance.

17. Think Before You Sext: Understanding the Consequences and Making Responsible Choices Online

Discuss the potential legal and emotional consequences of sexting and encourage students to avoid such activities.

Understanding the consequences of sexting is crucial for students to make informed decisions and protect themselves. It's important to educate them about both the legal and emotional implications of engaging in sexting activities.

From a legal perspective, students need to understand that sharing explicit content, even if consensual, can have serious legal consequences due to laws regarding child pornography, the distribution of sexually explicit material, and the potential for exploitation. Additionally, sexting can have detrimental emotional effects, including feelings of shame, regret, and damage to personal relationships.

Addressing sexting and inappropriate content also involves discussing the risks of sharing explicit or improper content via cell phones or other digital platforms.

Students should be aware that once a photo or video is shared, they lose control over how it may be further disseminated, potentially leading to cyberbullying, harassment, or public embarrassment. It is essential to emphasize the importance of consent and respect in all online interactions and encourage students to report any instances of inappropriate content they come across to trusted adults or the appropriate authorities.

By educating students about the legal and emotional consequences of sexting and discussing the risks associated with inappropriate content sharing, we empower them to make responsible choices, protect their privacy, and maintain healthy digital relationships. Open discussions create awareness, encourage critical thinking, and foster a safer online environment.

18.Be Smart About Online Advertising: Protecting Your Privacy and Making Informed Choices

Teach students to be skeptical of online advertisements and to avoid clicking on suspicious ads or providing personal information.

Teaching students to be skeptical of online advertisements is crucial for their online safety and privacy. They should learn to question the authenticity of ads, especially those that seem too good to be true or contain exaggerated claims. It is important to instruct students to avoid clicking on suspicious ads that may lead to potentially harmful websites or prompt them to provide personal information.

Students should also understand the significance of protecting their personal data and never share sensitive details through online advertisements. By instilling these principles, students can navigate the digital advertising landscape responsibly, protecting their privacy and ensuring a safer online experience.

19. Developing Critical Evaluation Skills: Navigating the Digital Information Landscape

Empowering students with critical evaluation skills is essential in the digital age. They should be taught how to assess the credibility and reliability of online information, particularly when conducting research. By fostering critical thinking skills, students can learn to question and evaluate the authenticity and credibility of content they encounter on social media platforms.

It's important to encourage them to seek out diverse perspectives, consider the potential impact of the content they consume on their mental well-being, and make informed judgments about the information they encounter online.

By equipping students with these skills, they can navigate the vast online landscape more effectively, make better-informed decisions, and become responsible digital citizens.

20. Encouraging Positive Online Content Creation: Fostering Digital Creativity and Responsible Citizenship

Encouraging positive online content creation empowers students to express themselves, showcase their talents, and contribute to the digital community in a meaningful way. Students can develop valuable skills such as creativity, critical thinking, and effective communication by guiding them in creating and sharing content that reflects their passions and interests. It's important to teach them about responsible digital citizenship, including respecting copyright laws, giving proper attribution, and adhering to ethical guidelines.

Emphasize the significance of creating safe, respectful, and inclusive content, fostering a positive online environment for themselves and others. By promoting positive content creation, students can harness the power of digital platforms to inspire, educate, and connect with others while positively impacting the online world.

21. The Impact of Social Media on Mental Health: Nurturing a Healthy Relationship with Technology

Educate students about the potential effects of excessive social media use on mental well-being and the importance of self-care.

Research findings consistently support the impact of social media on mental health, providing valuable insights for students. Heavy social media use has been associated with increased feelings of loneliness and social isolation, as well as higher levels of anxiety and depression among young people. Moreover, social media's promotion of unrealistic beauty standards often leads to negative body image and dissatisfaction. Comparing oneself to others on social media can also hurt self-esteem. Additionally, excessive social media use can disturb sleep patterns, affecting sleep quality. While the impact of social media on mental health can vary among individuals, these findings highlight the potential risks of excessive social media use. Educating students about these facts can empower them to make more informed decisions about their social media habits and prioritize their well-being.

22. Responsible Tagging and Sharing: Promoting Consent and Privacy in Online Interactions

Instructing students on the importance of obtaining consent before tagging others in posts or sharing their images or personal information is crucial in promoting respectful online behavior. Tagging involves identifying or mentioning someone in a post, photo, or comment on social media platforms. This act is typically done by using the individual's username, handle, or full name to associate them with a specific piece of content. However, it is vital to understand that tagging should be done with consent and consideration for others' privacy preferences. By seeking permission before tagging someone, we demonstrate respect for their boundaries and ensure responsible and considerate online conduct.

Empowering students to understand the consequences of liking inappropriate comments or pictures on social media is crucial in promoting responsible digital citizenship. Liking such content can tarnish one's reputation, perpetuate harmful material, have legal implications, and potentially compromise personal safety. Students need to realize that their online actions contribute to their digital footprint and can impact their future opportunities. Educating students about these consequences encourages them to make thoughtful decisions, prioritize their safety, and contribute to a positive online environment.

23. Building a Partnership for Online Safety: Involving Parents and Guardians

Involving parents and guardians in promoting online safety is essential for the well-being of students. By collaborating with parents and providing them with resources and workshops, we can empower them with the knowledge and tools needed to support their children in navigating the digital world safely. These initiatives can cover topics such as privacy settings, monitoring online activities, fostering open communication, and educating parents about the potential risks and challenges their children may face online. By working together, schools and parents can create a strong support system that reinforces safe and responsible online behaviors, ensuring the holistic protection of students in both their offline and online lives.

24. Promoting Responsible Cell Phone Use: Teachers as Role Models

As a teacher, being a role model for responsible cell phone use is crucial in guiding students toward respectful and accountable behavior. By demonstrating proper cell phone etiquette in the classroom, such as using phones only when necessary and avoiding distractions, teachers can set a positive example for students. Encourage students to follow your lead and emphasize the importance of using cell phones respectfully, considering their usage's impact on their learning and the learning environment. By promoting responsible cell phone use, teachers can help students develop healthy habits and better understand appropriate technology use in various settings.

25. The Dangers of Texting and Driving: Stay Focused, Stay Safe

It is crucial to emphasize the dangers of texting, driving, or using cell phones while operating any vehicle. Educate students about the potential consequences of distracted driving, such as accidents, injuries, and even fatalities. Stress the importance of keeping their full attention on the road and practicing responsible cell phone use while driving.

In addition to texting and driving, educating students about the dangers of texting and walking is equally important. Remind them that being distracted by their phones while walking can lead to accidents, falls, and collisions with objects or other pedestrians. Encourage them to be mindful of their surroundings and to prioritize their safety by keeping their eyes up and staying focused on their path.

By teaching students about the dangers of texting and driving and texting and walking, we can help them develop responsible cell phone habits and promote a safer environment for themselves and others.

PERSONAL SAFETY

PART 3

KEEP THEM SAFE

Part 3 – Personal Safety

Keep Them Safe: An Educators Guide to Personal Safety. Nurturing Empowered and Informed Students for a Secure Tomorrow

In an ever-changing world, the safety and well-being of our students stand as paramount concerns. As educators, parents, and guardians, our responsibility transcends traditional academic instruction. We are tasked with nurturing a generation that is not only intellectually empowered but also equipped with the skills and knowledge to navigate the complexities of life with confidence and resilience.

In this section of "Keep Them Safe: An Educator's Guide to School Safety, Digital Safety, and Personal Safety," we delve into a collection of 25 invaluable tips designed to empower students with a comprehensive Personal Safety mindset.

From the bustling hallways of schools to the wide-ranging landscape of the digital realm and the varied scenarios of personal encounters, these tips are carefully curated to address the myriad challenges students face in today's dynamic environment. My approach goes beyond mere caution; it's about instilling a sense of awareness, proactive decision-making, and personal responsibility.

Each tip encapsulates a critical aspect of safety, from prioritizing physical well-being and making informed choices to embracing digital savvy and mastering conflict resolution. I recognize that a holistic approach to safety encompasses multiple dimensions of life, and these tips guide fostering a well-rounded understanding.

Through these pages, you'll discover insights that range from guarding against potential dangers when wearing certain attire to harnessing the power of technology for personal protection. We address the significance of communication, the importance of trust in one's instincts, and the value of seeking support from a network of trusted individuals.

It's important to acknowledge that while we intend to equip students with the tools they need to navigate the world safely, we also understand that safety is a shared responsibility. Teachers, parents, guardians, and community members all play a role in creating an environment where students can thrive while feeling secure.

As you journey through these 25 tips, consider not only how they can be incorporated into your educational practices but also how they can be woven into the fabric of everyday life. By imparting these lessons, we aspire to shape a generation that is prepared, informed, and confident in its ability to prioritize safety in all its forms. Together, let's empower our students to stride forward with a safety mindset that enables them to embrace every opportunity in their educational pursuits and their journey through life.

1. Empowering Students with a Safety Mindset: Prioritizing Well-being and Making Informed Decisions

As a teacher, students need to have a safety mindset as it empowers them to prioritize their well-being and make informed decisions in various situations. Developing a safety mindset now offers several important benefits. Firstly, a safety mindset equips students with the knowledge and skills to identify potential risks and proactively protect themselves. It teaches them to be vigilant, assess their surroundings, and make informed choices that enhance their safety. By understanding and recognizing potential dangers. Students can take preventive actions, minimizing the likelihood of accidents or harm. This recognition empowers them with a sense of control and confidence in navigating different environments safely, fostering self-reliance and independence.

A safety mindset also ensures that students are prepared for emergencies. It instills a belief that they can protect themselves and make sound decisions, increasing their resilience and readiness to handle unexpected situations effectively. By learning about emergency procedures, evacuation routes, and proper responses to various scenarios, students are better equipped to respond appropriately in times of crisis. Moreover, developing a safety mindset at a young age establishes a foundation for lifelong safety habits. These skills extend beyond school settings and apply to various aspects of life, promoting their overall well-being and security. By instilling these skills early on, teachers enable students to navigate the world with confidence, preparedness, and a proactive approach to personal safety.

Through developing a safety mindset, teachers empower students to prioritize their well-being, make informed decisions, and respond effectively in various situations. By emphasizing the importance of a safety mindset and fostering its development now, students can acquire lifelong skills that contribute to their overall security and confidence.

2. Empowering Students with Personal Safety Awareness: Navigating Public Spaces and Responding to Emergencies

Teachers have a crucial role in empowering students to be personally safe by emphasizing the importance of staying alert and aware of their surroundings. This emphasis allows students to identify potential risks, make informed decisions, and take proactive measures to prevent harm. To enhance awareness, teachers can impart effective strategies such as minimizing distractions, engaging all senses to observe the environment actively, and regularly scanning for potential dangers. By doing so, teachers equip students with the necessary skills to prioritize personal safety and make sound choices in different situations, thereby enhancing their overall well-being.

Minimizing distractions is a key aspect of promoting awareness among students. Encouraging them to limit activities that divert their attention, such as excessive phone use or unrelated tasks, allows students to stay focused and attentive to their surroundings. Additionally, engaging all senses plays a vital role in enhancing awareness. Teachers can guide students to actively observe their environment by encouraging them to listen for unusual sounds, notice subtle changes, and trust their intuition or gut feelings. This comprehensive approach helps students develop a keen sense of their surroundings, enabling them to recognize potential risks or signs of danger quickly.

3. Empowering Student Safety: Enhancing Awareness and Response in Public Spaces and Emergencies

Teachers can empower students about personal safety by emphasizing key points about being aware of exits, emergency procedures, and evacuation routes in public places. Teachers can encourage students to develop situational awareness by actively observing their surroundings, identifying exits, and mentally mapping escape routes. By teaching them to pay attention to their environment, students can better anticipate and respond to potential dangers. Stress the importance of pre-planning and familiarizing themselves with emergency procedures in their school and other frequented public spaces. Encourage students to take the time to learn about evacuation routes and the location of emergency exits. This knowledge will enable them to respond quickly and effectively in an emergency. Emphasize the significance of being proactive and prepared, ensuring they understand the importance of navigating public spaces safely.

Teaching students to stay calm and follow instructions during emergencies is important, emphasizing effective communication and seeking assistance when needed. Discuss the importance of remaining calm and composed in stressful situations, as panic can hinder their ability to make rational decisions. Please encourage students to listen carefully to instructions from authorities or staff members and follow them promptly. Effective communication is crucial in emergencies, enabling students to express their needs clearly and seek help when required. Adaptability, problem-solving abilities, and teamwork can be achieved by discussing alternative options, fostering support for others, and cultivating a culture that values proactive safety measures. By providing students the tools to think critically and respond flexibly to unexpected situations, they become better equipped to handle emergencies and protect themselves and others. Encourage students to work together, supporting one another and promoting a sense of responsibility for the safety and well-being of the entire community.

4. Empowering Student Safety: Building Strong Communication Skills for Assertiveness and Conflict Resolution

Developing strong communication skills, including assertiveness and effective conflict resolution strategies, is essential for students to handle potentially unsafe or uncomfortable situations. These skills empower students to advocate for themselves and assertively express their needs, boundaries, and concerns. By confidently communicating their discomfort or asserting their rights, students are more likely to be heard and respected, thus reducing the risk of unsafe situations. They learn to set and maintain personal boundaries by clearly and respectfully expressing their limits, ensuring that others understand and respect their personal space and boundaries. This skill is crucial for avoiding potential dangers and navigating uncomfortable situations, allowing students to confidently assert their boundaries and say "no" when necessary.

Strong communication skills enable students to resolve conflicts peacefully and effectively. Teachers empower students to address potentially unsafe situations or disputes non-confrontationally by teaching them conflict-resolution strategies. These skills help students navigate difficult interactions, diffuse tense situations, and seek resolution without resorting to aggression or violence. Additionally, effective communication skills enable students to seek help and support when needed. Teachers ensure students can access the necessary support systems in potentially unsafe situations by teaching them how to articulate their concerns and seek assistance from trusted adults or authorities. This skill enables students to actively seek help, report incidents, and collaborate with others to ensure their safety and well-being.

By focusing on developing strong communication skills, including assertiveness and effective conflict resolution strategies, teachers equip students with the tools to handle potentially unsafe or uncomfortable situations. These skills foster self-advocacy, boundary setting, conflict resolution, and seeking help when needed, allowing students to assert their rights, establish personal boundaries, and ensure their safety in various contexts.

5. Exercising Caution: Safety Considerations When Wearing Expensive Clothing and Accessories

Wearing expensive clothing, including sneakers and jewelry, requires students to exercise caution to ensure their safety. Sporting expensive accessories can draw attention and potentially make individuals targets for theft or robbery. By being mindful of their clothing and accessories, students can minimize the risk of attracting unwanted attention and reduce the likelihood of becoming victims of crimes.

Sneakers and jewelry, in particular, can be highly valuable items and desirable targets for theft. Flashy sneakers or expensive jewelry may attract the attention of individuals with ill intentions. Students should consider their environment and assess the potential risks of displaying these items. They must make informed choices and decide whether wearing such things in certain settings is appropriate and safe.

Wearing expensive clothing and accessories can create a perception of wealth or privilege, leading to jealousy, envy, or negative interactions with others. This perception could result in confrontations or conflicts that jeopardize personal safety. Using caution and being aware of their surroundings; students can make informed decisions about when and where to wear expensive items, considering the potential implications for their safety and well-being.

6. Enhancing Personal Safety: The Importance of Keeping Electronics Out of Sight

Keeping electronics out of sight, such as phones and headphones, is crucial for students to enhance their personal safety in various ways. Firstly, visible electronics can target students for theft or robbery, as they attract unwanted attention. Displaying expensive devices in public spaces can draw the interest of individuals with malicious intent. By keeping these items out of sight, students reduce the risk of being targeted and minimize the chances of becoming victims of theft or other crimes.

Concealing electronics promotes personal privacy and minimizes distractions. Using or showcasing electronics in public can invite unwarranted interactions or distractions. By keeping these devices hidden, students can focus on their surroundings, maintain situational awareness, and avoid unnecessary attention that could compromise their personal safety. Moreover, hiding electronics also fosters a more secure learning environment. By minimizing the visibility of these devices, students are less tempted to use them during inappropriate times, allowing them to stay focused and fully engage in their academic pursuits.

7. Ensuring Personal Safety: The Significance of Letting Someone Know and Developing Safe Travel Habits

As a teacher, it is important to emphasize to students the importance of always letting someone know their whereabouts and developing safe travel habits. One effective way to achieve this is by utilizing family tracking apps, which can be used to stay connected with family and friends and ensure that someone is aware of their location. These apps provide an additional layer of security and peace of mind, allowing students to share their real-time location with trusted individuals who can assist in emergencies or unexpected situations.

In addition to using tracking apps, students should also develop safe travel habits. These safe travel habits should include informing someone, preferably a trusted individual, about their travel plans. By sharing their itinerary and expected arrival times, students ensure that someone is aware of their intended destination and can take necessary action if there are any concerns or delays. It is crucial to stress the importance of avoiding sharing detailed itineraries publicly, as this can inadvertently expose students to potential risks or unwanted attention.

Moreover, students should be encouraged to research safe transportation options. Finding safe transportation involves familiarizing themselves with reputable transportation providers and understanding the safest ways to travel in their local area or when visiting unfamiliar places. By doing so, students can make informed choices about the modes of transportation they use, prioritize their personal safety, and reduce the likelihood of encountering risky situations.

8. Locking Doors: Enhancing Personal Security and Promoting a Sense of Control

Locking doors is a primary defense against unauthorized access and potential threats, providing physical security for students' homes, dormitories, or personal spaces. By consistently locking doors, students create a barrier that helps prevent unwanted intrusions, ensuring their physical safety. Additionally, locking doors ensures privacy and establishes personal boundaries, empowering students to control who can enter their space and protect their privacy and personal belongings. This sense of ownership over their personal space fosters a greater understanding of security and control.

Moreover, locking doors deter potential crimes and help prevent incidents. When students understand the importance of locking doors, it sends a message that their space is secured, making it less attractive to potential intruders or opportunistic criminals. This simple action significantly reduces the risk of theft, home invasions, or other security breaches. By teaching students about locking doors, educators instill a sense of responsibility for personal safety and empower students to take proactive measures to protect themselves and their living spaces. This knowledge develops a mindset of self-reliance and active participation in maintaining personal safety and security.

9. Prioritizing Personal Safety at Parties: Drink Choices, Situational Awareness, and Responsible Decision-Making

When it comes to attending parties, students should prioritize their personal safety by making informed choices. One crucial tip to remember is to be cautious about drinking from cups you did not personally pour or witness being poured. This precaution helps minimize the risk of unknowingly consuming substances that could be harmful.

Instead, opt for unopened drinks, such as cans or bottles, as they are less likely to be tampered with.

In addition to being mindful of cups and drinks, it is important to maintain situational awareness at parties. Pay attention to your surroundings, observe the behavior of others, and trust your instincts. If something feels off or uncomfortable, removing yourself from the situation and seeking a safe space is essential. Having trustworthy friends who can support and look out for one another is invaluable in ensuring personal safety at social gatherings.

It is also crucial to be aware of the potential dangers associated with underage drinking. Engaging in underage drinking poses legal consequences and risks your health and well-being. Alcohol impairs judgment and can make you more vulnerable to accidents, assaults, or other hazardous situations. By making responsible choices and avoiding unknown cups, you reduce the likelihood of unknowingly consuming substances that could have harmful effects.

Remember, personal safety should always be a top priority. By being cautious about your drink choices, staying aware of your surroundings, and making informed decisions regarding alcohol consumption, you can enjoy parties while minimizing risks and ensuring a safe and enjoyable experience.

10.Enhancing Personal Safety: The Benefits of Changing the "Home" Location on Your Phone

Changing the home location protects their privacy by preventing potential strangers or individuals with malicious intent from easily identifying their exact residential address. By maintaining confidentiality, students reduce the risk of unwanted individuals accessing sensitive information about their homes. Additionally, this measure minimizes the chances of being tracked by location-based services, protecting against stalkers, thieves, or other perpetrators who may exploit their location data.

Altering the home location on their phone helps prevent targeted crimes and enhances online safety. Sharing their home location can make students potential targets for crimes such as burglaries or home invasions. Changing the home location makes it harder for criminals to identify their residential address, reducing the likelihood of being targeted. Moreover, displaying the home location on location-based services or social media platforms exposes students to risks like cyberstalking or identity theft. Changing the home location mitigates these risks by keeping their address private and allowing them to control who has access to their personal information.

Students can take proactive steps to protect their privacy, prevent targeted crimes, and enhance their online safety by understanding the significance of changing their phone's home location. It empowers them to have better control over their personal information and reduces the likelihood of being targeted by malicious individuals.

11. The Power of Trusting Your Instincts: Prioritizing Personal Safety for Students and Young Adults

Trusting your instincts is a powerful tool for students and young adults to prioritize their personal safety. Your intuition, often called the "sixth sense," can provide valuable guidance and protect you from potential risks. Here's why it's important to trust your instincts and be prepared to take action when feeling uncomfortable or threatened:

Your instincts act as immediate warning signals, alerting you to potential dangers that may not be immediately apparent. As a student or young adult, paying attention to feelings of unease or gut instincts that tell you something is not right is crucial. Trusting your instincts empowers you to prioritize your well-being and personal safety. By listening to your inner voice and acknowledging your discomfort or sense of threat, you can take appropriate action to remove yourself from potentially unsafe situations. This action may involve speaking up, seeking help from a trusted adult or authority figure, or physically distancing yourself from the environment.

Trusting your instincts also helps you develop a heightened awareness of your surroundings and the people you interact with. It encourages you to be more observant, attentive, and attuned to subtle cues and behaviors that may indicate potential risks. Additionally, it fosters assertiveness, empowering you to advocate for yourself, set boundaries, and assert your rights in situations that make you feel uneasy or threatened. When you trust your instincts and act accordingly, you build self-confidence in navigating challenging situations. You reinforce your self-trust and belief in your judgment by honoring your intuition and making choices aligned with your inner guidance. This self-assurance extends beyond personal safety and positively impacts other aspects of your life, such as decision-making, relationships, and overall well-being.

Remember, trusting your instincts is a valuable skill for students and young adults to stay safe and make informed decisions. Cultivate this innate ability by paying attention to your feelings, listening to your gut instincts, and taking proactive steps to remove yourself from unsafe or uncomfortable situations. Doing so empowers you and enhances your safety and overall well-being as you navigate your academic and personal journey.

12. Empowering Student Safety: The Importance of the Emergency SOS Feature on Smartphones

Knowing how to use the emergency SOS feature on your smartphone is important for students. It provides immediate access to help in emergencies, allowing them to quickly connect with emergency services such as the police, ambulance, or fire department. By activating the SOS feature, students can alert responders and provide vital information about the emergency and their location, ensuring that help arrives promptly with the necessary resources and support.

The emergency SOS feature enhances personal safety by providing a direct and streamlined communication channel. Students can quickly and efficiently convey their situation without lengthy conversations, enabling a faster response from emergency services. This tool empowers students to take control of their safety, giving them the confidence to handle emergencies and be prepared for unexpected events.

Regularly practicing the use of the emergency SOS feature further strengthens preparedness. Students should become familiar with this process and can act swiftly in need. Additionally, the SOS feature is widely available on most modern smartphones, making it accessible to students in various settings, whether at school, out with friends, or traveling.

Knowing how to use the emergency SOS feature on a smartphone is crucial for students. It ensures immediate access to help, enhances personal safety, promotes empowerment and preparedness, and is widely available. Students can proactively protect themselves and others during emergencies by equipping themselves with this knowledge.

13.Safeguarding Personal Space: The Importance of Verifying Front Door Visitors

Students should understand the importance of verifying who is at their front door as it directly relates to their personal safety. By confirming the identity of visitors, they can assess potential threats and protect themselves from harm. Verifying front door visitors is a preventive measure to prevent unauthorized individuals with malicious intent from entering their homes. It enables students to make informed decisions about opening the door, allowing them to prioritize their security and well-being. This practice is particularly important for children and young adults to learn, as it instills a sense of caution and empowers them to take ownership of their safety.

In addition to assessing potential risks, verifying front door visitors gives students control over their personal space. It empowers them to decide who can access their home environment, enhancing their sense of security. To ensure the safety of themselves and their families, students can evaluate the situation by verifying the identity of visitors. This practice fosters a vigilant mindset, reducing the likelihood of falling victim to potential threats or scams. It also encourages the adoption of additional security measures, such as peepholes, doorbell cameras, security cameras, or intercom systems, further enhancing the overall safety of their homes. By developing a habit of verifying front-door visitors, students cultivate a proactive approach to personal safety and create a safer living environment for themselves and their loved ones.

14. Prioritizing Personal Safety: The Importance of Refusing Rides from Strangers

Students should never accept rides from strangers, no matter what, as it is a fundamental aspect of personal safety. By refusing rides from strangers, students establish a strong boundary that reduces the risk of encountering danger or potentially harmful situations. Accepting a ride from a stranger increases the risk of abduction and exposes students to unknown intentions. Predators often offer a ride to lure unsuspecting individuals, especially vulnerable children or teenagers. By teaching students to reject rides from strangers, they can protect themselves from potential abduction attempts and avoid compromising their safety.

In addition, choosing not to accept rides from strangers helps students to develop their own judgment and decision-making abilities. It fosters independence, self-reliance, and the ability to navigate their surroundings confidently. Students learn the importance of setting personal boundaries and prioritizing their well-being by establishing a firm rule of not accepting rides from strangers. This lesson extends beyond transportation and helps them develop assertiveness and self-preservation skills that can be applied in various aspects of their lives. By emphasizing the significance of this rule, educators equip students with the knowledge and awareness to make responsible decisions and protect themselves from potential harm.

15. Staying Safe: What to Do When Being Followed by a Stranger

As a concerned teacher and parent, your students must know what to do if a stranger follows them. First, they should stay calm and trust their instincts. Please encourage them to take the situation seriously and not ignore any feelings of discomfort or suspicion. Next, instruct them to seek a safe and populated area immediately. They should move towards well-lit places, stores, or establishments with other people around. They should consider going to an alternative location, such as a neighbor's house, where they can seek refuge and contact a trusted adult.

Also, teach your students to avoid confronting the person following them. Confrontation can escalate the situation and potentially put them in harm's way. Instead, they should maintain visual awareness of the follower without drawing attention to themselves. Remind them to gather details such as the person's physical appearance, clothing, or any distinguishing features that could be useful for the authorities. Furthermore, emphasize the importance of contacting a trusted adult promptly. Please encourage them to use their cell phone to make the call. Finally, remind your students to report the incident to the appropriate authorities, such as the school administration or the local police. Prompt reporting can aid in identifying patterns, providing descriptions, and ensuring the safety of your students and the community.

16. Keeping Valuables in Sight: Enhancing Personal Safety and Responsibility

Encouraging students to keep their valuables in sight and not leave them unattended is crucial for personal safety. There are several reasons why this practice is important. First, students significantly reduce theft risk by keeping their belongings within sight. Personal items like phones, wallets, headphones, and laptops can be tempting targets for opportunistic thieves, and keeping them in view makes them less vulnerable.

Secondly, teaching students to keep their valuables in sight instills a sense of personal responsibility. It empowers them to take ownership of their belongings and prioritize their safety. When students actively keep their possessions within sight, they become more aware of their surroundings and are less likely to become victims of theft or loss.

Furthermore, promoting the habit of keeping valuables in sight fosters a culture of trust and mutual respect within the school community. Students who understand the importance of personal responsibility are less likely to accuse others of theft or engage in dishonest practices themselves. This responsibility creates a safe and supportive learning environment where everyone can focus on their education without unnecessary distractions.

Lastly, developing the habit of keeping valuables in sight is relevant during school hours and prepares students for situations in other public places. Keeping their belongings within sight becomes second nature, whether at a library, a coffee shop, a fast food restaurant, or a park. This habit ensures that students are mindful of their personal safety wherever they go, reducing the likelihood of becoming a victim of theft or losing their valuables.

17. Empowering Students Through Information: Enhancing Personal Safety in School and Community

As a teacher, students must stay informed about information and news in school and town for their safety. Firstly, being aware of school-related information such as safety protocols, emergency procedures, and updates on potential risks or hazards helps students understand how to respond appropriately in different situations. By staying informed, students can be prepared and take necessary precautions to ensure their safety within the school environment.

Similarly, staying informed about news and events in their local community is essential for personal safety. Local news can provide important information about security threats, weather conditions, or other emergencies that may impact the community. Students aware of these updates can adjust their plans accordingly, avoid potentially dangerous areas, or take appropriate actions to stay safe.

Additionally, encouraging students to sign up for school and local emergency alerts further enhances their safety. By subscribing to these alerts, students can receive timely notifications about emergencies, lockdowns, severe weather warnings, or other critical information. These notifications enable them to stay informed and take immediate action to protect themselves and others.

Overall, staying informed about information and news in school and town is crucial for students' personal safety. It empowers them to make informed decisions, be prepared for emergencies, and take necessary precautions to mitigate risks. By promoting a culture of awareness and encouraging students to sign up for emergency alerts, teachers play a vital role in ensuring the safety and well-being of their students.

18. Maintaining Awareness: The Importance of Headphone Usage for Personal Safety

When students venture out in public, it is crucial to exercise caution and avoid using over-ear headphones or listening devices that block their ability to hear. Additionally, it is important to refrain from blasting music at excessively high volumes. These devices can hinder one's awareness of the surrounding environment and pose potential risks to personal safety.

Over-ear headphones can isolate individuals from ambient sounds, making it difficult to hear important cues or warnings, such as approaching vehicles, sirens, or people's conversations. By opting for open-ear or in-ear headphones instead, students can enjoy their music while maintaining their ability to hear external sounds. These headphone types enable them to stay alert and respond promptly to potential dangers or emergencies.

Similarly, having music or audio content playing excessively loud can impede one's ability to hear important sounds in the environment. Students need to keep the volume reasonable to allow them to enjoy their music while remaining aware of their surroundings. The appropriate volume ensures they can hear potential warnings, announcements, or other auditory signals contributing to their safety.

Students can enhance their situational awareness in public spaces by avoiding over-ear headphones and maintaining a moderate volume level. This heightened awareness empowers them to make informed decisions, navigate potential hazards, and stay safe. It is crucial to prioritize personal safety by being mindful of headphone usage and loud music's impact on one's ability to hear and respond to their environment.

19.Prioritizing Safety: Avoiding In-Person Meetings with Online Acquaintances

When it comes to online interactions, students need to understand the importance of never agreeing to meet up with someone they meet online. Regardless of how friendly or trustworthy someone may appear, exercising caution and prioritizing personal safety is crucial.

Meeting with strangers online can be risky, as verifying their true intentions or background is difficult. People may present themselves differently online than in person, and their intentions may not always be genuine or safe. Students can mitigate the potential risks of meeting unknown individuals by avoiding in-person meetings with online acquaintances.

Refraining from engaging in extensive conversations with strangers online is equally important. While connecting and interacting with others through social media or online platforms is natural, students should exercise caution and avoid sharing personal information or engaging in conversations that may compromise their safety or privacy.

By adhering to the principle of not meeting up with online acquaintances and exercising caution in online interactions, students can protect themselves from potential risks and maintain their personal safety. It is vital to prioritize personal well-being and engage in responsible online behavior to ensure a safe and secure online experience.

20. Promoting Personal Safety through Responsible Transportation Practices

Practicing responsible use of transportation is crucial for personal safety in various scenarios. Here are some key aspects to consider:

Wearing Seat Belts in Vehicles: Wearing seat belts is one of the most effective ways to protect oneself while traveling. Students should be educated about buckling up, whether driving or riding as passengers. Seat belts significantly reduce the risk of injury or fatality in a collision or sudden stop. Please make sure students are aware of seat belt laws in their state.

Using Designated Crosswalks when Walking: When walking near roads or intersections, it is essential to use designated crosswalks whenever available.
Crosswalks provide a safer passage for pedestrians by ensuring that they cross at designated locations with the assistance of traffic signals or markings. Crosswalks help increase drivers' visibility and reduce the risk of accidents or collisions.

Following Traffic Rules when Cycling: Students who ride bicycles should know and adhere to traffic rules and regulations. These rules include obeying traffic signals, riding in designated bike lanes or paths whenever possible, signaling turns, and yielding to pedestrians. By following these rules, cyclists can enhance their safety and contribute to the overall safety of the road.

Practicing responsible use of transportation reduces the risk of accidents and injuries and promotes a culture of safety and consideration for others; by wearing seat belts, using designated crosswalks, and following traffic rules when cycling, students demonstrate their commitment to personal safety and contribute to a safer transportation environment for everyone.

21. Empowering Students and Young Adults through Substance Awareness: Prioritizing Health, Well-being, and Personal Safety

Students and young adults should be aware of the potential risks and dangers associated with drugs, alcohol, and tobacco to prioritize their health, well-being, and safety.

Here's why this awareness is crucial:

1. **Informed Decision-Making:** Understanding the risks and dangers associated with substance use allows students and young adults to make informed decisions. They learn about the potential negative impact on their physical and mental health and the risks of addiction, impaired judgment, and risky behaviors. This information empowers them to weigh the short-term gratification against the long-

term consequences and make choices that safeguard their overall well-being.

2. **Personal Safety:** Awareness of the risks associated with substance use helps students and young adults prioritize their safety. They can recognize situations where their judgment may be compromised, leading to vulnerability and unsafe circumstances. By being informed, they can make responsible choices such as avoiding environments that involve substance use, refusing offers of drugs or alcohol, and surrounding themselves with supportive and trustworthy peers who also prioritize health and safety.

3. **Building Healthy Habits:** Knowing the potential risks and dangers of drugs, alcohol, and tobacco encourages students and young adults to develop and maintain healthy habits. They can adopt alternative ways to cope with stress, peer pressure, and emotional challenges, reducing the inclination to use substances as an escape or coping mechanism. This understanding empowers them to develop resilience, emotional intelligence, and effective strategies for managing difficulties without relying on harmful substances.

4. **Peer Influence and Support:** When students and young adults know the risks, they can positively influence their peers and promote a culture of well-being and personal safety. By sharing their knowledge and experiences and making responsible choices, they advocate for a healthy lifestyle. This peer influence and support system creates an environment where everyone values health, well-being, and safety.

In conclusion, students and young adults should be aware of the risks and dangers associated with drugs, alcohol, and tobacco to prioritize their health, well-being, and personal safety. This awareness enables them to make informed decisions, prioritize personal safety, build healthy habits, and positively influence their peers. Understanding the risks allows them to navigate challenges more effectively, cultivate resilience, and create a supportive environment that encourages a healthy and safe lifestyle.

22.Promoting Safe Walking Practices: Choosing Well-Traveled Routes for Student Safety

Students should be encouraged to avoid walking alone in isolated or poorly lit areas and opt for well-traveled routes whenever possible due to several important reasons. Firstly, walking alone in remote areas increases the risk of becoming a target for potential threats, such as theft, assault, or harassment. By avoiding these areas and choosing well-traveled routes, students are more likely to be in the presence of others, which can serve as a deterrent to potential perpetrators and provide a sense of safety.

Secondly, poorly lit areas can significantly decrease visibility, making it harder for students to identify potential hazards or react to dangerous situations effectively. By opting for well-lit routes, students enhance their ability to observe their surroundings and be aware of any potential risks. Increased visibility helps them stay alert and proactive in their personal safety and increases the likelihood of others noticing and coming to their aid if needed.

Furthermore, using well-traveled routes offers the advantage of increased social surveillance. When students choose paths frequently taken by others, there is a higher chance of encountering fellow students, pedestrians, or residents. This presence of people provides a form of natural surveillance, where others can potentially intervene or offer assistance if a student finds themselves in an uncomfortable or unsafe situation.

Ultimately, by avoiding walking alone in isolated or poorly lit areas and utilizing well-traveled routes, students can significantly reduce their vulnerability to potential risks and enhance their safety. Encouraging this behavior empowers students to make informed decisions about their routes, consider their surroundings, and prioritize their well-being when moving from one location to another.

23. Seeking Help from Trusted Adults: Empowering Personal Safety and Well-being

Students should know that if they are unsure about a personal safety issue, seeking help from a trusted adult or authority figure is important. This action can greatly contribute to your well-being and overall safety. Trusted adults, such as parents, teachers, counselors, or mentors, are there to support and guide them through difficult situations.

When unsure about a personal safety issue, reaching out to a trusted adult allows them to gain perspective and advice from someone with more experience and knowledge. They can provide reassurance, help you assess the situation, and offer guidance on the best course of action. Their wisdom and insights can empower them to make informed decisions prioritizing their safety and well-being.

Additionally, seeking help from a trusted adult or authority figure helps you build a support system. These individuals can connect you with additional resources or professionals specializing in personal safety and well-being. They can also advocate on your behalf and ensure appropriate measures are taken to address any concerns or risks the students may face.

Remember, asking for help when unsure about your personal safety is never a sign of weakness. It demonstrates strength and maturity to recognize when you need guidance or support. By reaching out to a trusted adult, you are taking an important step toward protecting yourself and ensuring your overall well-being.

24. The Power of a Support Network: Promoting Health, Well-being, and Personal Safety

Developing a support network of trusted friends and peers is crucial for students and young adults to prioritize their health, well-being, and personal safety. This network offers several benefits that contribute to their overall protection and growth. Firstly, a support network provides mutual protection by looking for each other's safety. Friends and peers who genuinely care can intervene in potentially risky situations, provide support, and help prevent harmful behaviors. A reliable support system instills a sense of security and confidence when navigating different environments.

Additionally, a strong support network offers emotional support during challenging times. Students and young adults often face various stressors, and having trusted individuals who can provide a listening ear, advice, or comfort is invaluable. This network promotes mental health, resilience, and a sense of belonging. Furthermore, a support network allows for the sharing of knowledge and experiences. Students and young adults can exchange information about personal safety, healthy habits, and effective strategies for dealing with difficult situations. By learning from one another, they develop a broader understanding of potential risks and gain insights into making informed decisions. Ultimately, a support network provides accountability and positive influence. Trusted friends and peers encourage responsible choices, motivate each other to engage in healthy behaviors, and hold one another accountable. This culture of care fosters personal growth and helps individuals align their choices with their values and well-being.

25. Empowering Students Through Emergency Contact Numbers and Helplines: Promoting Preparedness, Independence, and Safety

Students must familiarize themselves with emergency contact numbers and helplines, keeping them readily accessible for several reasons. Firstly, it promotes emergency preparedness by equipping students with the knowledge of whom to contact during critical situations such as accidents, injuries, or dangerous incidents. Students can quickly seek help when needed by having these numbers readily available. Secondly, in today's digital age, where students rely heavily on their phones, they need alternative means of communication. Memorizing emergency contact numbers and helplines provides students with a backup plan in case of phone loss, theft, or technical issues. They can utilize public phones, borrow devices from others, or seek assistance to reach out for help when necessary.

In addition to emergency preparedness and accessibility, familiarizing students with emergency contact numbers and helplines fosters independence and self-reliance. It empowers students to take ownership of their safety and well-being by encouraging them to be proactive and responsible for their protection. Calling important contacts in emergencies enhances self-reliance and reduces dependency on others. Moreover, this knowledge holds lifesaving potential. In critical situations requiring immediate medical attention or intervention, knowing whom to call can significantly reduce response time, increasing the chances of a positive outcome. By encouraging students to keep these numbers readily accessible, teachers ensure that students have the means to reach out for necessary help during crises.

Dr. Raymond Trigg was a highly experienced and respected police officer with over 27 years of service. In addition to his work in law enforcement, he has also dedicated himself to education and teaching, serving as an adjunct professor at several institutions.

Throughout his career, Dr. Trigg has worked to promote personal safety and has implemented numerous programs to reach and educate children about the dangers of drugs and gangs.

He holds a Bachelor of Science degree in Administration of Justice, a Master of Arts degree in Human Resource Training and Development, an Educational Specialist degree in Educational Leadership Management and Policy for Law Enforcement, and a Doctorate of Education in Higher Education. He's a loving husband and father of three amazing kids.

Become a Safety Partner and help Dr. Trigg Spread the word by visiting: **DrRaymondTrigg.com**